ZIPPY
AND THE
VERY BIG COOKIE

by Carla Golembe

But Zippy does not know how to make a cake. And he only has a *recipe for cookies.

Zippy does not want cookies. He wants a cake.
He decides to make one very big cookie. That will be just like
a cake.

Zippy puts eggs in a bowl.

He puts in butter.

He adds a cup of sugar.

He adds flour and chocolate *chips and mixes everything with a spoon.

He *pours it into a dish.

Zippy puts the dish in the *oven. His big cookie will be ready in
forty minutes.

After ten minutes Zippy looks inside the oven. The cookie is getting bigger.

After twenty minutes the cookie smells good. The cookie is even bigger now. It is taller than the dish.

"What a big cookie," says Zippy.

After thirty minutes when Zippy looks inside the oven, the cookie is so big he can't see the dish at all. "What a very big cookie!" says Zippy. "It's good I'm hungry."

After forty minutes Zippy is really hungry. He can't wait to eat his big cookie. But when he goes to take it out of the oven he cries, "Oh no!"

The very big cookie is pushing open the door of the oven.

Zoe tells Zippy, "There is a piece of cookie between your ears."

Zippy and Zoe eat all the pieces of the cookie.

"Now I'll teach you how to make a cake," says Zoe.

生字表

n.=名詞，prep.=介系詞，v.=動詞

賽皮與超級大餅乾

p.3

一個下雨的午後，賽皮肚子餓了，他決定烤個蛋糕來吃。

p.4

但是賽皮不會做蛋糕，而且，他只有做餅乾的食譜可以看。

p.5

賽皮並不想吃餅乾，他想吃蛋糕，所以他決定做一個超級大餅乾，大到像一個蛋糕一樣。

p.6

賽皮在碗裡打了一些蛋。

p.7

又放了一些奶油。

p.8

再加上一杯糖。

p.9

然後他倒入麵粉和巧克力碎片，用湯匙把所有的東西攪拌在一起；

p.10

最後把它倒在烤盤上。

p.11

賽皮將烤盤放進烤箱裡烤。四十分鐘後，他的大餅乾就會完成了。

p.12

十分鐘過後，賽皮往烤箱裡看，發現那塊餅乾變大了。

p.13

二十分鐘過後，餅乾散發出香味，而且又變得更大了。它現在比烤盤還要高。
賽皮說：「這塊餅乾真大。」

Author's Note

This is based on a true story. When I was a little girl, my friends and I decided we wanted to bake one very big cookie. We mixed everything up, poured it into a cake pan and baked it. It exploded all over the oven.

作者的話

「賽皮與超級大餅乾」來自一個真實的故事。當我還是個小女孩時，我和我的朋友決定要烤一個超級大餅乾。我們把每樣東西都混合在一起，把它倒進一個裝蛋糕的盤子裡，然後拿去烤。結果它爆炸了，弄得整個烤箱都是。

About the Author

Carla Golembe is the illustrator of thirteen children's books, five of which she wrote. Carla has won several awards including a New York Times Best Illustrated Picture Book Award. She has also received illustration awards from Parents' Choice and the American Folklore Society. She has twenty-five years of college teaching experience and, for the last thirteen years, has given speaker presentations and workshops to elementary schools. She lives in Southeast Florida, with her husband Joe and her cats Zippy and Zoe.

關於作者

Carla Golembe 擔任過十三本童書的繪者，其中五本是由她寫作的。Carla 曾多次獲獎，包括《紐約時報》最佳圖畫書獎。她也曾獲全美父母首選基金會，以及美國民俗學會的插畫獎項。她有二十五年的大學教學經驗，而在過去的十三年中，曾經在多所小學中演講及舉辦研討會。她目前和丈夫 Joe 以及她的貓——賽皮與柔依，住在美國佛羅里達州東南部。